MW01681428

RAISING THEM REBUILDING ME

A Memoir of Motherhood, Trauma, and Healing

Kimberly Miller Wynne

This book is a personal memoir based on the author's lived experiences and memories. Some identifying details have been omitted, altered, or generalized to protect the privacy of individuals referenced in this work. The author has not used full names for family members, friends, or other persons mentioned.

Descriptions of events, locations, and institutions—including hospitals and cities—reflect the author's personal recollections and perspectives.

Contents

Dedication

For my children—

my heart, my joy, and my greatest inspiration.

Your laughter, resilience, and love have given

my life meaning in every season.

Every step I took, every chapter I survived,

and every hope I held onto was for you.

This memoir exists because you existed first

in my heart.

What I carried became the strength

that carried me forward.

— Kimberly Miller Wynne

Author's Note

This memoir was written from memory, and from the body that carried it. The experiences shared in these pages reflect my personal recollection of events as I lived and understood them at the time. Memory is not a fixed record; it is shaped by age, emotion, trauma, and growth. What I have written here is my truth—not the only truth, but the one that belongs to me. Others who appear in this story may remember certain moments differently, and that difference does not invalidate either experience.

Some identifying details have been changed or omitted to protect the privacy of individuals referenced throughout this memoir. I have chosen not to use full names for family members and others, not to obscure the emotional truth of the story, but to respect boundaries that extend beyond my own life. The purpose of this book is not exposure or accusation—it is understanding.

This memoir is not written to place blame. It is written to bear witness.

For much of my life, survival required silence. I learned early how to endure pain quietly, how to keep moving forward without fully naming what I carried. Writing this book meant breaking that silence—not dramatically, but deliberately. It meant revisiting moments of trauma, resilience, motherhood, loss, and healing with honesty instead of avoidance. It also meant acknowledging how deeply the body remembers what the mind sometimes tries to forget.

Motherhood sits at the center of this story—not as a backdrop, but as a force that shaped every choice I made. I raised children while learning how to raise myself. I rebuilt my life while carrying responsibility, grief, and hope all at once. This memoir reflects that duality—strength and exhaustion, devotion and doubt, love and loss existing side by side. Some chapters may be difficult to read. They were difficult to write. Still, I chose to include them because healing does not come from omission—it comes from truth. I believe there is power in naming what we survive, especially when so many women are taught to endure quietly and move on without being seen.

This book does not claim resolution. It does not offer a neat ending or a perfected version of healing. Instead, it honors the ongoing process of becoming—of learning how to live beyond survival, how to grieve without disappearing, and how to choose softness without surrendering strength.

If you see yourself reflected in these pages—your pain, your perseverance, your longing to be whole—I hope you feel less alone. This story is offered not as instruction, but as companionship.

Preface: Between Breaking and Becoming

I never set out to write a book. I set out to survive.

Writing came later—after the chaos quieted just enough for me to hear my own thoughts again, after years of putting one foot in front of the other and rebuilding what I had lost, piece by piece. When people ask why I decided to write, I usually smile and say, *"It wasn't really a decision. It was a release."* For a long time, survival was my only goal; living, healing, and reflecting came afterward.

My journey has not been neat or easy. It has been beautifully imperfect—marked by both heartbreak and healing. I have navigated unreturned love, profound heartbreak, and moments of isolation so deep I feared I would never find my way back to myself. Yet I have also known joy—the quiet, unexpected kind that arrives when you least expect it, reminding you that you are still here, still breathing, still capable of feeling beyond pain.

This memoir is not a story of perfection. It is a story of persistence—of rebuilding after trauma, of raising children while learning how to rebuild myself. It is about finding hope in the ruins and realizing that sometimes the most broken parts of us are the ones that let the light in.

It is also about my children—the greatest teachers I have ever had. They have shown me what resilience looks like in motion, what forgiveness feels like in practice, and how love can stretch far beyond fear. Watching them grow has been both humbling and healing. They are my living reminders that every scar, every stumble, and every restart holds meaning.

If you have ever felt broken, this story is for you.
If you have ever looked in the mirror and wondered whether you were enough, I have been there.
If you have questioned your beauty, your worth, or your belonging—I have too.

I share these pages not for pity, but for connection. I do not want sympathy; I want understanding. Because maybe you have been invisible too. Maybe you have carried pain no one else could see—smiling when it hurt, trying to be strong because the world told you that was your only option.

You are not alone.
You are not invisible.
And you are stronger than you think.

This memoir is my offering to every woman who has ever rebuilt herself from the inside out—who has juggled motherhood and heartbreak, who has tried to heal while still showing up for others. It is proof that scars can coexist with softness, that grace can grow out of grief, and that beauty is not the absence of damage; it is the courage to live openly in spite of it.

When I first began writing, I did not realize how hard it would be to tell the truth—to truly tell it. There were drafts that ended in tears and moments when I considered deleting everything because it revealed too much. But I kept going. Silence never saved me, and I refuse to let it silence anyone else.

This story is offered with the hope that it might help someone else know they are not alone.

Introduction

I was born into a family of ten children in a little town called Java, Virginia. If you blinked while driving through, you would miss it—just a couple of winding roads, a handful of houses scattered between fields and woods, and neighbors who recognized the sound of your car before they ever saw your face. Growing up there meant living inside a bubble of both love and limitation. Word traveled fast in our small town; everyone had an opinion. But it also meant community—people who checked on you when you were sick and looked after you when your parents were stretched too thin, which, in a house of ten children, was often.

Ours was a home full of sound—laughter carrying through the hallways, arguments erupting over chores or who got the last biscuit, and the hum of everyday life that rarely stood still. We did not have much, but what we had, we shared. There was always a pot on the stove and a story to tell. My siblings and I learned early how to negotiate, how to hold our ground, and how to disappear into the background when needed. There is an art to being one of ten; you learn to adapt quickly or be swallowed by the noise.

For the youngest four of us—my twin and my other two brothers—childhood meant work as much as play. All ten of us shared daily chores: collecting eggs, feeding animals, and tending the garden, where we picked string beans, corn, and whatever else was in season. Even the smallest tasks taught us responsibility and patience, shaping who we were long before life tested us in harsher ways.

But for all its noise and life, home could turn silent in an instant.

When I was just two years old, that silence came after a scream—a sharp, splitting sound that seemed to stop time itself. A tragic accident left me with second-, third-, and fourth-degree burns covering much of my body. My twin brother suffered second-degree burns on his back. His injuries were less severe, so he did not remain in the hospital as long as I did, though he spent time there as well. I do not remember the pain—only what my family later told me: the rush of hands trying to help, my mother's face terrified but strong. When my grandmother arrived at the hospital from Delaware, she prayed over me and continued even after she left.

I was too young to understand any of it. I only knew that my body felt like evidence—of an accident, of survival, of being seen before I was known. That awareness settled in quietly, shaping how I learned to stand, to move, and eventually, to protect myself.

People sometimes say trauma builds character. I do not believe that is true. Trauma breaks you. What builds character is what you choose to do after the breaking—the small, stubborn decision to keep showing up for your own life. My burns healed over time, but the lessons they left behind did not fade. They taught me that pain does not have to define you, but it does have the power to refine you. Pain strips away illusions, teaches humility, and reveals the depth of your endurance.

Growing up in Java, I learned early that strength was not loud or showy. It was quiet, steady, and often unseen. It was my mother rising before sunrise to prepare meals for her children. It was my father, who worked in Washington, D.C., coming home on weekends and doing his best to provide. It was my older siblings stepping in when someone faltered. And later, it was me—learning how to rebuild myself after every setback, one quiet act at a time.

As I grew older, the world beyond our small town began to call to me, whispering promises of independence and reinvention. I wanted more than survival; I wanted purpose. I wanted to build a life my younger self—the girl with burns on her right arm, both legs, stomach, and ankle—would be proud of. That desire became my compass, even when life pulled me in directions I did not expect, especially when motherhood arrived long before I felt prepared for it.

With motherhood came babies to care for, household responsibilities to manage, and a spirit that refused to give up, no matter how many times it was tested. Even then, I found moments of grace: a child's laughter in the next room, a late-night conversation with a friend, the simple relief of a sunrise that meant I had made it through another night.

My journey since then has not been about perfection; it has been about persistence. About rebuilding myself while raising them. About learning that even when life breaks you down completely, you can rise again—not the same, but stronger, wiser, and unafraid to tell the truth of what it took to get here.

Over time, I learned that the body remembers what the mind cannot. Long before I had words for fear or resilience, my body was already responding—flinching before danger, bracing itself in unfamiliar spaces, carrying a quiet vigilance that became second nature. I did not yet understand that this was survival, not weakness. I simply knew that I was always listening, always aware. As I grew, that awareness became both armor and compass. It taught me when to retreat and when to stand firm, when to soften and when to protect what mattered most.

Slowly, almost without noticing, I began to trust myself—not because life had been gentle, but because I had endured it. And in that trust, I found something even stronger than survival: the ability to live fully, honestly, and without apology for the scars that tell my story.

Some beginnings arrive through pain, not choice. What matters is not how the story starts, but that it continues.

Chapter 1 — Scars of the Beginning: The Day Everything Changed

☼

The day everything changed did not announce itself. There was no thunder, no warning, no sign from heaven. Just the quiet heartbeat of a small Virginia morning, the low rumble of an ancient refrigerator, the hiss of boiling water, the smell of string beans and salt curling into the kitchen like a lazy ribbon.

Ordinary days are often the ones that hold the most power. Nothing about that morning suggested it would fracture my life into before and after. It was simply a moment suspended in routine—the kind of moment that teaches you later how fragile normalcy really is.

My mother moved between the stove and sink, humming an old song she always hummed when she cooked, a tune older than her memory, older than mine. Then, in a single unguarded moment, everything turned to heat.

That song, though I cannot recall its melody, lives on as a symbol of what was lost in that instant. Comfort. Safety. The illusion that home is always gentle. What followed rewrote those assumptions in ways I would spend years trying to understand.

I was small enough that the world still existed as shapes and sounds rather than meaning. My twin brother and I had discovered that the oven door made a perfect step for climbing. The stove stood on a stack of bricks to keep it level on the uneven kitchen floor, and to us it looked like an adventure waiting to happen.

Childhood curiosity has no concept of consequence. We didn't yet know about danger. We didn't know that the objects meant to nourish could also harm. We only knew movement, balance, and the excitement of discovery.

Bare feet on cool linoleum, eyes bright with curiosity, we were explorers of our own tiny kingdom. We didn't yet know about danger. We didn't know a pot of hot water could become deadly in the time it takes to blink. All we knew was balance, the sway beneath our feet, the thrill of height—and then, suddenly, the world tipped.

The bricks slipped. The stove lurched. My mother later told me there was a sound like thunder inside the house, a low metallic groan followed by a crash that seemed to swallow the air. The pot toppled and for half a second hung there, suspended mid-fall as if the whole world held its breath. Then gravity took over. The water spilled. It rushed down. And then came the pain.

Pain, at that age, has no narrative. It is raw sensation—overwhelming, consuming, and immediate. It does not ask permission. It simply arrives and demands everything.

I was told that I screamed, though I don't remember it. I was too young. What I know now came from my mother's trembling recollection when I was older. She told me my twin brother screamed too—his voice high with fear and confusion—and that together, our cries filled the kitchen.

The smell was thick and sickly sweet, like sugar burning on a hot skillet, mixed with the metallic bite of steam and something else she said she couldn't name at the time. My own skin.

That detail—the smell—is one my mother still cannot forget. It followed her long after the kitchen was cleaned, long after the towels were washed. Trauma, I would later learn, imprints itself in ways no amount of time can fully erase.

My mother's voice cut through the chaos, loud and breaking. She called our names over and over, as if the sound alone could undo what had just happened. She later told me she scooped us both up in towels, our small bodies trembling against her chest, and called for help, trying to keep her voice steady. I vaguely remember the rough texture of the towel and the blur of movement as we were carried outside. The image that remains sharpest is the look on the ambulance driver's face—an expression that seemed to say, "Oh my goodness," as he saw what had happened.

They rushed us to the small hospital in Halifax, Virginia. Doctors pulled back the sheet and froze for an instant when they saw what the boiling water had done. My mother told me later that the acrid scent of burned cloth and flesh filled the air. They moved fast with oxygen masks and IV lines and barked orders, but what I remember most from her retelling is the bite of air on my wounds and her voice somewhere out of sight, breaking apart with every sentence.

They knew I was too badly burned. Within minutes, they called Richmond for a MedFlight helicopter.

The rest is a blur of motion—the thrum of the helicopter engine, footsteps, faces swirling around my small body. When they lifted me onto the stretcher, my body stiffened—or so I've been told. My mother later said the medical staff pressed a mask over my mouth, and the ceiling seemed to spin away as they lifted me toward the helicopter.

After that, I was flown to a burn center in Richmond, Virginia, where I would remain for six grueling months. The physicians told my mother not to expect me to survive. Second-, third-, and fourth-degree burns covered my right arm and both legs, stomach, and ankle. My toddler's frame had to relearn the simple tasks of living. For weeks, I refused to eat, shrinking into a shadow of myself. I was kept alive through medical feeding, but I would not take food on my own.

Later, I was told that one day one of my brothers opened a bag of barbecue potato chips nearby, and the smell made me reach for one. It was the first thing I chose to eat—the small moment that signaled I was coming back to life. My family waited in vigil, clinging to hope that I would somehow pull through.

My grandmother prayed incessantly—long, shuddering prayers whispered at dawn, repeated at midnight, breathed into the thin pages of her Bible when she thought no one was listening. She prayed louder when the doctors advised my mother to prepare for the worst.

And somehow, through the quiet, the agony, and through death's steady pull, I clung to life.

Healing was not kind. Burns are hard teachers; they don't just mark skin—they mark every sense, every sound, every breath. My earliest memories are of white walls, humming fluorescent lights, and the sharp smell of iodine that clung to my sheets.

I was wrapped like a doll in heavy bandages that made my body stiff and awkward. When the nurses changed those bandages, the air struck my raw skin like knives. There was no way to soften it. The bandages had to come off; the dead tissue had to be scrubbed away so new skin could grow. Each time felt like the first. I could feel my pulse inside the wounds, each throb a reminder that I still existed.

The nurses worked briskly, their voices steady, their eyes holding compassion they tried not to show. I remember the clink of metal basins, the hiss of the faucet as they filled tubs with water. They would lower me into those tubs so the dead skin could slough off. The water looked smooth, almost inviting, until the first touch. Then came the pain—burning, cutting, obliterating the world except for the sound of my own cries.

Afterward, they would lift me out, wrap me in fresh white gauze, and whisper that I was getting better. My body didn't feel like my own anymore. It was the 1980s when I was burned, and at that time, thermoplastic splints and orthoses were used to prevent contractures—the tightening or shortening of the skin as it healed. My limbs were bound in thermoplastic splints to keep the new skin from pulling tight. The sound of those straps ripping open each morning still haunts me.

They kept my arms and legs stretched so I wouldn't curl into myself, so my body wouldn't freeze in its own defense. The burns on my right leg were the worst. They had eaten through muscle and tissue until walking became a memory, not a possibility. My body's instinct was to fold, to protect, to hide from the pain. But the therapists wouldn't let me.

Physical therapy was a battlefield. I would cry, beg, and refuse, but they kept going. "One more step, Kimberly," they'd say. "You can do this." Step by trembling step, I fought my way back. The pain was a living thing, but so was my stubbornness.

Even once I was released at last, the hospital remained with me. The appointments continued unabated. Checkups. Therapy. Additional procedures. I learned the cadence of waiting rooms, the sound of nurses' heels on tile floors, the manner in which people's eyes lingered on mine when they looked at my skin.

I became a sort of curiosity—half child, half warning. Some adults would smile too brightly, their pity gleaming through their courtesy. Others would look away, as if not seeing. Either way, I could feel their stare like a burden on my shoulders.

Outside, I was the girl with splints, the girl with scars, the girl who survived. They never told me "miracle" to my face, but I heard it in their whispers.

I learned to walk again, though each step served as a reminder of what it had cost. The flesh pulled taut over my joints; the scars itched and pounded as they healed. Some nights I awoke sobbing, convinced I could still feel the water cascading down. But I persevered. I persisted. Because somehow, against all odds, I remained standing.

When I was five, the doctors told my mother it was time to start kindergarten.

Other kids waited for school to begin with pencils, crayons, naptime, and new sneakers. The first day of school is supposed to be exciting—a brand-new, shiny backpack, sharpened pencils, a kiss on the forehead from your mother as she lets go of your hand.

For me, it was a day of terror.

I remember standing in the doorway of the classroom, grasping my mother's hand like a lifeline. The smell of chalk and crayons was familiar yet foreign. Reds and yellows covered the walls, colors that ought to have made me smile, but all I could feel was the pounding of my heart. I wasn't afraid of the alphabet or the teacher's rules. I was afraid of being seen.

I recall holding a small backpack and gazing at the classroom door, hoping the other kids would not notice. My scars had healed but never disappeared. My skin was uneven, spotty, and dark in areas where the burns had devoured deep. My right knee remained stiff, and I continued wearing the supports beneath my clothing.

To me, it was simply my body—the one and only I had ever had. To everyone else, it was a show.

Walking into that bright classroom, a buzz of talk surrounded me, but I sensed the stares before seeing them. Children gazed without ill will, only curiosity. Their whispers echoed through the room like a breeze. I wanted to disappear, to fade into the pinstripe of the floor. But my feet felt rooted to the floor.

Children notice everything. They do not mean to be cruel; they are exploratory. But when their gaze settled on me, I sensed it like a spotlight. They stared at my scars. Their small brows furrowed as if trying to solve an enigma.

"What's wrong with you?" one girl finally asked, her voice small but clear enough to echo in the quiet room.

The question sliced through me. I opened my lips, but the words stayed there. How could I define hospitals and bandages, scars and physical therapy, when I barely understood them myself? How could I explain the scent of antiseptic that still clung to me, or the sensation of my own skin feeling too tight, too new, too exposed?

I did not know how to utter any of these things. So I said nothing.

My mother's hand closed harder around my own—a silent reminder that I owed no one an explanation. But shame had already scaled up the back of my throat. I didn't look up at anyone; instead, I focused on the floor and my shoes—polished patent leather, the sole unbroken part of me.

It was my first lesson about how the world looks at difference—not as a survival story, but as something to question and gawk at. In that moment, I knew that the scars I had weren't just on my skin; they were inscribed into the way people looked at me.

That afternoon in the kitchen years ago had defined it all—my body, my confidence, my sense of home. My skin held the memory of scalding water and survival, of what it is to be marked in a world that treasures smoothness.

Even as a child, I felt the gravity of that difference. I did not yet possess the vocabulary of trauma and resilience, but I knew what it was to be stared at, pitied, and spoken about.

But that day also meant something else.

It meant the start of my tale of survival.

It was the beginning of learning how to live inside a body that told a story before I ever opened my mouth. Survival, I would learn, is not a single moment of triumph—it is a series of quiet decisions made over a lifetime. It is choosing to show up on days when the mirror feels like an adversary, when memory seeps into muscle and bone, when the past hums just beneath the skin. I did not yet understand that my life would require a different kind of bravery—one that asked me to remain visible in a world uncomfortable with scars.

As the years unfolded, I learned how to move carefully between wanting to disappear and needing to be seen. I learned how to read a room before entering it, how to anticipate questions before they were spoken, how to armor myself with silence when words felt too heavy. But I also learned something else, something just as powerful: that survival could grow into strength, and strength into purpose. My scars did not vanish with time; they softened, stretched, and changed, just as I did. And slowly, almost imperceptibly, they became less about what had been taken from me and more about what had been preserved.

That first day of school was not just an introduction to classrooms and chalkboards—it was my initiation into a lifelong negotiation with the world. A lesson in difference. A lesson in endurance. A lesson in the quiet courage it takes to keep standing when you would rather fold inward. I did not know it then, but I was already practicing resilience. Already beginning the long, patient work of reclaiming my body, my voice, and my story.

And though I could not yet name it, that day marked the moment I began learning not just how to survive—but how to live.

Before I learned who I was, the world decided what it could see. It took years to unlearn the lie that appearance tells the whole story.

Chapter 2 — Skin Deep: What the World Could See

☼

Kindergarten was only the beginning.

By the time I was old enough to stand in front of a mirror and truly study myself, I already knew I was different. It wasn't just the scars—though those were always the first thing people noticed. It was something deeper, something I could feel long before I had words for it.

The stares had become background noise, following me everywhere—from classrooms and church pews to grocery store aisles, where mothers pulled curious toddlers closer when their gazes lingered too long. Even when I pretended not to notice, the staring found its way into me. It hummed quietly in my chest, a reminder that I was being seen before I was being known. I learned how to lower my eyes, how to move quickly through rooms, how to take up less space so the attention might pass me by. I didn't realize then that shrinking myself would become a habit I'd carry for years.

But there was another kind of gaze that cut differently. It wasn't about the burns. It was about my skin. My color.

I was dark-skinned, darker than most of my classmates, darker even than some members of my own family. And though I didn't yet have the language for colorism, I could already feel its quiet sting—in the way people spoke, in the way they smiled, and in the things they didn't say but made sure I noticed anyway.

Colorism didn't announce itself loudly. It whispered. It disguised itself as preference, as concern, as "helpful advice." It lived in comparisons that sounded harmless and jokes that were meant to be funny. Even when no one said the words outright, my body learned the lesson anyway.

I saw how lighter skin was praised—how girls with honey- or caramel-toned skin were called "pretty," how their hair drew more compliments, how their nicknames were "sweet" and "cute." I listened to the way adults' voices softened when they spoke to them and realized early that certain shades came with privileges: invisible, unspoken, but powerful.

I didn't understand why, but I felt it. I saw it in the way teachers chose which students received attention during morning announcements, the way store clerks offered smiles to one child but silence to another. Even my friends compared skin tones like trophies—joking that one was "just right" while another was "too dark."

And then it reached home—from the one person I loved and trusted most.
My mother.

She wasn't trying to hurt me. I know that now. Back then, it only confused me. She was passing down lessons carved into her by a world that had once made her feel small for the same reasons. She had her own quiet wounds and believed she was protecting me from hers.

"You should use this cream," she told me one evening, her voice soft and practical. "It'll help even out your skin. Make it smooth."

Her words weren't cruel; they were careful, almost tender—the kind of advice that sounded like love because it was meant that way. She was teaching me how to survive in a world that wasn't always kind to dark girls. At home, I wanted refuge from the world, but the world followed me there too, tucked inside well-meaning guidance and inherited fear.

Bleaching creams—"even-tone" products—lined our bathroom counter in bottles and jars, shiny with promises to fade dark spots and brighten complexion. My mother handed them to me like tools for self-improvement, small defenses against judgment. "It'll help you look your best," she'd say.

And I believed her, because daughters are born believing their mothers.

So I rubbed the creams into my cheeks and

forehead, watching as my melanin reacted, leaving uneven patches of red and brown. The scent was sharp, chemical, nothing like the gentle lotions my classmates used. Sometimes it stung. Sometimes it left my skin raw and dry, tingling like tiny sparks beneath the surface. But I endured it—waiting for change, waiting to see if the girl in the mirror would finally resemble the ones who received praise.

Each night became a ritual. I imagined a future version of myself—lighter, smoother, chosen. I thought maybe if I could change enough on the outside, the inside would quiet down. Maybe God would finally answer my prayers in the mirror.

And every night I lingered a little longer in the bathroom, sometimes collapsing to the floor, praying to God to make me pretty. I was tired—tired of the teasing, tired of hearing,

"Boy, you sure aren't pretty!" I wondered if the world would ever see me differently, or if I would always be the only one waiting for my reflection to change.

But the darkness didn't disappear.

My face stayed mine—uneven in tone, still dark, unchanged. The mirror never lied; it reflected a stubborn truth: no cream could erase what the world had already decided about girls like me.

I remember standing on my tiptoes at the sink, the harsh light buzzing above me, tracing the places where I thought my skin should have looked "better." The creams promised transformation, but all they delivered was irritation and tight dryness that cracked when I smiled. Instead of feeling prettier, I felt more flawed—like my reflection was a wall I couldn't climb, a reminder that the world's judgment had already written itself across my face.

The little jars returned to the shelf each night like soldiers guarding an impossible dream. My mother's eyes would rest on me, hopeful.

"It takes time," she'd say.

And I'd nod, pretending to believe her. But deep down, I knew time wasn't the problem. It was me.

The creams didn't heal me. They reminded me of everything I wasn't—or thought I wasn't. Each sting, each tingle, each breath of that sharp chemical smell whispered that there was something wrong with the way God had made me, something I had to fix before the world could love me.

What I really wanted wasn't lighter skin.

I wanted to be enough.
I wanted to enter a classroom without hearing the hush that followed me.
I wanted to sit at lunch without the half-hidden glances or quiet whispers.
I wanted to raise my hand without wondering if my scars or my skin made me the wrong kind of girl.
I wanted to look in the mirror and not feel like I was failing at being me.

The boiling water had scarred my body, but colorism scarred my spirit. One told me I had survived. The other told me survival wasn't enough.

Slowly, I began to believe the lie—taught not just by classmates or magazines, but by the world—that lighter was better and darker was less. It settled into me quietly, like dust gathering in corners: unnoticed at first, but always there. Even without the vocabulary, I carried its weight like an invisible bruise beneath my skin.

By eleven or twelve, the rituals of self-correction had become habit. The bottles of cream no longer felt foreign on my dresser; they were part of my nightly routine, lined up neatly beside my barrettes and combs like silent witnesses to my insecurity.

Every evening, I stood before the mirror, rubbing the creams into my skin, praying that maybe tomorrow I would wake up lighter.

Every morning, the mirror responded with truth.

My face stayed mine.
My skin refused to change.
The darkness I had been taught to resent remained loyal to me.

I carried it as failure, long before I understood it as a kind of grace.

But it wasn't just my skin that drew comparison—my hair soon joined the battle.

For years, my mother's hands were the first to touch my hair. Later, my older sisters or the neighborhood braider took over. My hair was short then, just long enough for small, neat braids. I wished it would grow thick and long, imagining that maybe then I wouldn't be teased.

They parted my hair carefully, fingers moving rhythmically, tugging gently as they wove each braid. The soft clinking of bracelets became part of the pattern—a small song of care disguised as routine. Those nights were ours, with television murmuring in the background, the air thick with the scent of Blue Magic grease, and their patience stretching well past exhaustion.

But as I got older, the mirror reflected comparisons I hadn't sought—girls on television with hair that swung and shimmered, girls in my class who could run fingers through theirs without resistance. The world had already decided what beauty was worth noticing, and I wanted desperately to belong.

My first salon visit felt like entering another world—the hiss of dryers, the clatter of combs, the sound of women's chatter mixing with Motown on the radio. It smelled like sugar and smoke, a blend of pressing oil, relaxer, and dreams.

Sitting in that chair, I felt both nervous and important. The stylist ran her fingers through my thin hair, then pulled the hot comb from the stove, its teeth glinting gold. She pressed it through my hair section by section—steam rising, a faint whiff of singed strands curling upward.

Then came the relaxer.
Then the Curly Kit—the Jheri curl.

Each one a promise.
Each one a disappointment.

My reflection became a revolving door of experiments, each style carrying fragile hope: maybe this version of me would be the right one.

But while I experimented with myself, the world experimented with me. Kids at school didn't hold back—they never do.

"Let your soul glow!"
"You Black and ugly."
"Gapped-tooth."

Each insult landed like a stone, layering itself over the ones already etched beneath my skin.

I was too dark.
Too scarred.
Too gap-toothed.
Too much of everything they didn't want.
Not enough of anything they did.

The creams, the chemicals, the teasing—they made me feel like my entire body was an experiment in correction. What I didn't yet understand was that the real problem wasn't my reflection. It was the world that insisted I needed to change.

The bleaching creams.
The salon trips.
The Jheri curls.
The rituals of war against myself—all of it became my normal.

By thirteen, I was exhausted from fighting battles I couldn't win.

That's when I discovered weaves.

At first, they were practical—hiding thinning patches and protecting what little hair I still had. But soon, the weave became something else entirely.

It was armor.
It was control.
It was the only place where I could decide how the world would see me.

The salon became my sanctuary—the rhythm of chatter, the buzz of clippers, the sharp scent of hair glue, the tug of braids stitched tightly to my scalp. The stylist transformed me strand by strand, and when I walked out, I felt lighter somehow, my confidence woven into every piece of hair.

For a few hours, I could pass for normal. I could walk the hallways without hearing whispers. I could look at myself without flinching.

Even then, I knew the truth: no style could heal what hurt beneath the surface. But weaving gave me something I desperately needed—a sense of control in a world that had already taken too much from me.

By the end of seventh grade, my body, my hair, my skin—every inch of me—carried the marks of survival. They told a story even when I didn't speak.

I didn't yet have the language for empowerment or healing. But I was beginning to understand dignity. It was in the way I held my head high when I wanted to shrink. It was in the way I smiled even when it hurt. It was in the stubborn act of showing up to life again and again, despite what it had taken from me.

Because surviving wasn't only about enduring pain—it was reclaiming the right to see beauty in myself, not despite the scars but because of them.

By the time middle school arrived, the world I had built around scars, creams, weaves, and careful observation had given me something precious: a sense that I could survive.

But surviving didn't mean I knew how to live.

Not yet.

Some wounds leave scars you can point to. Others settle quietly inside you, shaping how you trust, how you fear, and how you survive.

Chapter 3 — Shadows of Childhood: Early Wounds and Lasting Impact

☼

By the time I crossed the threshold into middle school, I had already learned how to survive scrutiny. I knew how to read faces, how to brace myself for laughter disguised as humor, how to armor my spirit before the day even began. My body had become a map of lessons learned too early—each scar, each ritual, each silence marking where innocence had been interrupted. I carried myself carefully, as though balance alone might keep me from falling apart.

What I did not yet understand was how much that vigilance would cost me. Staying guarded meant staying tense. Protection left little room for softness. My shoulders were always tight, my stomach knotted, my thoughts circling worst-case outcomes before anything had even happened. I had learned how to endure pain, but not how to recognize safety when it appeared—or how to trust it long enough to let myself rest inside it.

Middle school was where the watching changed. Curiosity hardened into expectation. Compassion thinned. Strength was no longer admired—it was assumed. I was expected to handle more, carry more, absorb more without complaint. And I did. I showed up each day stitched together by habit and determination, convincing myself that this was what resilience looked like.

I was still standing. Still surviving. Still performing the careful balance I had mastered so young. But beneath that steadiness, something in me was withdrawing. I laughed when I was supposed to. I smiled when it was safest. I kept my fears neatly folded, hidden beneath hairstyles and practiced confidence, unsure where they could be set down without consequence.

I did not yet know the language of trauma or healing. I did not understand that survival, practiced long enough, can begin to feel like confinement. I only knew that living inside constant alertness was exhausting, and that no amount of preparation could fully protect me from what I could not yet name.

Middle school would be the place where endurance stopped being enough. Where the wounds I carried quietly would begin to shape how I trusted, how I feared, and how I learned to move through the world.

Middle school brought new challenges, less visible than scars or ointments, yet ones that would shape how I understood trust, fear, and the quiet strength required to endure what others could not see. From elementary school into middle school, I was learning how to live inside a body that carried stories other people did not understand. My scars came with me everywhere—down hallways, into classrooms, and into the lunchroom. No matter how much I smiled or laughed, they followed me like shadows I could not shake.

Every day felt like a balancing act between wanting to blend in and learning how to stand tall in my difference. The teasing never fully stopped, but I began finding small ways to carve out space for myself—quiet corners where I could breathe, moments where I could simply exist without being the girl everyone whispered about.

My mother tried, in her own way, to help me build a world beyond the stares. She signed me up for piano lessons and dance classes, saying I needed "something beautiful to focus on." I did not realize then how deeply she understood that beauty could be a form of healing.

Piano became my refuge.

The lessons did not take place in a fancy studio or quiet music room; they happened in our living room. Somehow, my mother had made it work, finding a way for us to have a piano in the house. That small upright instrument became a sanctuary, a place where the world outside did not exist.

My teacher was strict and unrelenting. She criticized mistakes sharply and expected perfection at every lesson. At the time, it felt almost cruel. Looking back, I recognize the discipline she instilled. The lessons were demanding, uncomfortable, and often frustrating—but they forced me to focus, to listen, and to push myself beyond what I believed I could not do.

At first, the piano felt impossible. The notes confused me, my fingers felt clumsy, and my teacher's critiques left me doubting myself. I did not believe I could master even the simplest pieces. But week by week, I proved myself wrong. I memorized difficult passages. I played songs without mistakes. I felt sparks of pride take root. Each small success became evidence that I could endure—that my body and mind were capable of more than I had believed. In that living room, the piano became a bridge between survival and the beginnings of living.

Dance became another language.

At the only dance academy in South Boston, Virginia, I took tap, ballet, and jazz classes. Acrobatics was off limits; my right knee, affected by the burns, could not handle it. At first, I was shy and unsure of how my legs should move or how far I could push myself. But movement silenced doubt. Each tap step, pirouette, and jazz combination gave me a sense of control over my body that I had not felt before.

Dance pushed my physical abilities in ways I had never imagined. After enduring rigorous physical therapy at such a young age, I had underestimated what my body could do. Moving in rhythm, spinning across the studio floor, leaping despite hesitation—it all felt exhilarating and freeing. With every rehearsal, I felt something return to me: grace, strength, and confidence in my physical presence. My body, once a source of shame, revealed itself as capable of rhythm, power, and beauty.

Those afternoons of piano lessons and dance were not just after school. They were small acts of rebellion—proof that my body was more than scars and creams. It was an instrument of expression and joy.

Music gave me wings.

In middle school, I joined the band and played the clarinet. Performing at concerts and school events, I felt my presence rise above the crowd—part of something larger than myself. The rhythm, the harmony, the shared purpose—it made me feel connected and capable. With each performance, I felt a growing sense of belonging. I mattered.

Friendship became my lifeline.

I gravitated toward friends who did not notice my scars first. They saw my laughter, my stubbornness, my music, my drive. They cheered during band performances, clapped wildly after piano recitals, and danced beside me at school events without hesitation. With them, I felt safe. I felt normal.

Their kindness did not erase the pain I carried, but it softened it. They reminded me that I could be seen and valued for who I was—not for what had happened to me. Those friendships became proof that I was not invisible.

That summer, childhood slipped further away.

Something darker had happened—a violation that left me anxious, raw beneath the surface.

I didn't have words for it. No one asked.

The stress didn't stay quiet. It lived in my stomach, in my outbursts, in restless nights spent replaying things I didn't understand. My body learned fear before my mind learned language.

It was meant to be simple—a few weeks in Maryland helping one of my siblings by babysitting. My mother believed it would be good for me: a change of scenery, a little responsibility. It was family, a place where I should have felt safe.

But safety disappeared.

While I was there, a family member I trusted violated me. He was part of our family by marriage. It happened quickly, yet it froze time. My body went still while my mind tried to escape. I did not understand what was happening or why. I only knew that something inside me had shattered.

When I returned to Virginia, nothing looked different, but everything had changed. I carried shame and confusion like a second skin. I moved quietly, smiled less, and pretended everything was normal. Pretending felt safer than trying to explain something I could not yet understand.

About three weeks after coming home, the truth surfaced.

One afternoon, I stood in the kitchen ironing. My mother and I argued—I was sharp, frustrated, and disrespectful. In anger, she threatened to send me back to Maryland.

That was the moment I broke.

I remember the iron trembling in my hand as tears fell. I begged her not to send me back, and the words spilled out before I could stop them. I told her why. I told her what had happened. I told the truth I had carried in silence.

After that, my mother ensured the situation was addressed. I was taken seriously. I received counseling. But even with support, I no longer loved myself. I sank into depression, overwhelmed by shame, anger, and unanswered questions. Therapy helped, but healing was slow. This became another wound layered atop many others—a setback that made me feel as though I were starting over.

For a long time, I believed silence was protection. I told myself that staying quiet would shield my family from guilt, protect me from doubt, preserve the little girl still frozen in that moment. But silence turns inward, and it began to consume me.

Prayer became my private language.

When I could not speak to anyone else, I spoke to God. I did not ask for miracles—only peace, sleep, relief from the weight pressing on my chest. Those prayers marked the beginning of forgiveness—not for what was done to me, but for the silence I once believed was necessary.

In time, I learned the truth: what happened was not my fault. The little girl I had been deserved safety, love, and protection. That understanding came slowly, but it came.

The violation left an invisible scar—one no amount of weaves or smiling could conceal—but it did not define me. It became part of the fabric of my story, shaping how I learned to trust again, how I found my voice, and how I came to understand what true resilience looks like.

With every hardship, I was building

something. Each scar, each lesson, each quiet act of survival laid another stone in the foundation of the woman I was becoming.

Strength did not arrive all at once. It came in fragments—every time I stood up, even when I wanted to disappear.

Chapter 4 — Rising Through Challenges

☼

High school felt like stepping onto unfamiliar land—not threatening, but strange—haunted by whispers I had not yet learned to quiet. What happened in middle school disturbed something deep inside me, and I carried that rupture into freshman year as an invisible wound. My scars, my hair, my skin—all of them held stories I was not ready to carry openly, including the innocence that had been taken from me. High school did not ask what I carried; it simply expected me to keep moving.

The first day of ninth grade was hot, the kind

of Virginia heat that clings to clothing. I stood in the bathroom mirror that morning, comb in hand, pressing down stubborn hairs and smoothing the weave I had done myself the night before. The mirror was no longer just glass; it had become a quiet witness to the changes I was trying to make. My reflection looked back at me with cautious hope. I did not know if I approved of what I saw, but I was learning to meet my own eyes without flinching. That alone felt like progress.

The hallways smelled of waxed floors and nervous energy—hundreds of students brushing past one another, laughter echoing, shoes squeaking across tile. No one knew what had happened to me the year before, and anonymity felt like both a blessing and a loneliness. I wanted to blend in, to be just another teenager worried about homework and crushes—not the girl with scars up her legs and secrets pressed into her chest. But life rarely offers that kind of simplicity. Instead, it asked me to carry both visibility and invisibility at once.

If I could not silence the noise in my head, I decided I would drown it out with music. After school, I sat at the piano in our living room and played. Those moments became my sanctuary—a place where melody replaced chaos, where small victories mattered, where belonging did not have to be earned. The piano never questioned me. It did not judge. It simply responded to my touch, meeting me exactly where I was.

Dance remained part of my life. I still loved the deliberate movement, the control, the grace I could command. Though my right knee was no longer mentioned as an obstacle, the lessons it had taught me stayed close.

Each plié and step became a quiet affirmation of who I was becoming. Dance showed me that strength did not have to be loud—it could be precise, measured, and steady.

Hair, however, was its own battleground. My relationship with it was complicated—half pride, half defense. Weaves boosted my confidence when they were flawless, but they also served as armor, something I hid behind when bravery felt out of reach. I learned what my hair could withstand: which products burned, which styles survived humidity and long school days. I became my own stylist—patching, brushing, fixing—each act small but defiant. In those moments, I felt capable. In control of at least one thing.

Sometimes a curl slipped loose or a track showed near my crown. I would duck into the bathroom between classes, fumbling with black hair glue, trying to fix it before anyone noticed. But teenagers notice everything. By the time I returned to my seat, whispers had already traveled the room. Their glances reminded me how fragile perfection was—and how closely scrutiny followed.

There were moments I wanted to disappear. But I never let them see me cry. Instead, I lifted my head, fixed my hair later, and kept walking. Each small repair became an act of resilience, a refusal to let someone else decide how I felt about myself. Strength, I was learning, often looked like composure.

Even then, I craved belonging. I searched for spaces where I could be seen for more than what marked me on the surface. I gravitated toward people and places that allowed me to exhale.

High school was far from perfect. The teasing

never vanished, and the stares never fully stopped. But between music, movement, and small personal victories, I began carving out something that resembled confidence. I learned how to advocate for myself—how to ask teachers for extensions, how to walk into a room without apologizing for existing. These were not grand transformations, just quiet shifts that accumulated over time.

Slowly, the fragments of me—the frightened child, the scarred girl, the guarded teenager—began to fit together again. My body remembered pain, but it also remembered rhythm, laughter, and light. Memory, I learned, is layered; it holds hurt and hope at the same time.

By sophomore year, the trembling uncertainty beneath my skin began to quiet. I no longer woke up dreading my reflection. Instead, I recognized the person looking back—still healing, still learning, but standing taller than before. Familiarity replaced fear.

Sophomore year marked the moment resilience stopped being a label others used for me and became something I claimed. I grew deliberate about who I allowed close. Gossip and shallow connections no longer appealed to me. I wanted depth. I wanted people who could meet me without flinching at my truth. I learned that intimacy required discernment.

Not everyone deserved access to my softness. I began setting quiet boundaries—resting when I needed to, walking away when jokes crossed lines, protecting memories from careless hands. It was not bitterness. It was self-respect.

Music and dance continued to carry me. The

piano understood my moods better than anyone. Some afternoons, I played until the sunlight faded, letting melody measure the passing hours. In those moments, I felt whole.

By junior year, I had found a rhythm. I was not popular, but I was respected—the kind of respect that grows from consistency, effort, and quiet resolve. Teachers noticed. My grades improved. My confidence expanded. The walls I had built began to open, cautiously. Trust returned in measured doses.

There were still difficult days—offhand comments that stung, reflections that triggered old insecurities. But those moments no longer ruled me. I learned to let them pass without letting them take root. I did not deny the pain; I refused to live inside it.

By senior year, I knew who I was, even as I continued discovering who I wanted to become. I made choices that nearly derailed me, but I found my way back. The trauma from middle school had not disappeared; it lived quietly beneath my decisions, shaping how I trusted and loved. Some friendships were unhealthy, and I learned to release them.

I was not alone. A teacher noticed when my smile did not reach my eyes. A guidance counselor asked, "Are you really okay?" and waited for the truth. Friends showed up with milkshakes after rehearsals, reminding me that laughter still belonged to me. Their presence mattered more than they knew. And there was my mother—always watching, always praying. She never pushed too hard, but she reminded me of what she had already taught: survival is only the first step. Living comes next.

Senior year was not a fairy tale. There were arguments, heartbreaks, sleepless nights. But there was also joy—pep rallies, prom nights, late drives with music too loud and windows down. Ordinary moments became sacred because they proved I was still here.

Graduation arrived on a warm June morning. The gym smelled of polished floors and anticipation. The gown rested heavy on my shoulders; the tassel brushed my cheek under bright lights. I saw my mother's face, my father's, my twin brother—even though he had not graduated with me—and siblings who came despite complicated paths. I smiled until it hurt. For the first time, the applause did not feel like pity. It felt like victory.

High school tested me physically, emotionally, spiritually. It refined me. I learned that resilience is not a single act—it is the daily choice to show up for yourself, even when no one else sees the effort.

College waited ahead like a blank canvas. For the first time, I was not afraid of what might fill it. I carried what high school taught me: independence, self-worth, forgiveness, and the courage to begin again. My scars remained, but they no longer felt like endings. They were punctuation marks in a sentence still being written.

That summer, before college, I sat at the piano one last time in my childhood home. The keys were worn, the bench creaked, sunlight spilled through the curtains. I played the same song that had once carried me through fear. The notes were softer now—not from sadness, but from understanding what healing sounded like.

I was no longer just surviving.

I was learning how to live.

Living, I discovered, was quieter than survival. It did not announce itself with urgency or adrenaline. It arrived slowly, in ordinary moments that once would have gone unnoticed. It was choosing rest without guilt. It was laughter that came easily instead of defensively. It was waking up without immediately bracing for harm. These changes were subtle, but they were real. They marked a shift I could feel in my body before I could articulate it in words.

The girl who entered high school armored and alert did not disappear; she softened. She learned when to hold her ground and when to let go. She learned that strength could coexist with tenderness, that protection did not have to mean isolation. The habits that once kept me safe—constant vigilance, emotional restraint, self-monitoring—began to loosen their grip. In their place grew something unfamiliar but welcome: trust in my own resilience.

I did not mistake this for completion. Healing was not a finish line I had crossed, but a rhythm I was learning to keep. Some days I moved easily; other days I stumbled back into old patterns. But I no longer punished myself for that. I was learning patience—not just with others, but with myself. Growth, I realized, is rarely linear. It circles, revisits, and deepens.

As high school ended, I felt the pull of what came next. College represented freedom, but also responsibility. No longer would structure be handed to me; I would have to choose it. No longer would survival be enough; intention would be required. I stood at the edge of adulthood aware that the wounds I carried had shaped me—but determined they would not confine me.

What I took with me was not just resilience, but discernment. I knew my limits. I knew my triggers. I knew the cost of silence and the danger of shrinking. I also knew the power of music, movement, and honest connection to anchor me when the world felt unstable. These were not small tools; they were lifelines.

High school had taught me how to stand. What came next would teach me how to step forward.

Freedom is not the absence of struggle. It is learning who you are when no one is watching.

Chapter 5 — College: New Beginnings

☼

College felt like stepping into an entirely new world, one where I could finally explore who I was without the lingering shadows of teasing, scars, and old judgments. For so many years, I had been in survival mode—learning to adapt, learning to keep going no matter what life threw my way. But college was different. It wasn't about surviving anymore. It was about living.

I followed in my older brother's footsteps when I left home for college. Knowing he had gone before me made the idea of leaving feel possible, even when fear tried to creep in. He graduated after my freshman year, and suddenly the campus felt much larger—but by then, I had begun learning how to stand on my own.

The day I arrived on campus, the air was alive with movement and noise—cars unloading boxes, laughter spilling through open dorm windows, and the smell of freshly cut grass mixing with the faint scent of cafeteria food. For the first time in my life, I wasn't defined by what people thought they knew about me. I wasn't the girl with the burns or the girl who'd been through too much. I was just me, a young woman stepping into her own story, one class, one moment, one new experience at a time.

The first semester of freshman year was a whirlwind of excitement and nervousness. I remember lying awake the first night, the hum of distant conversations drifting through the hallway, realizing that this was the beginning of something that belonged entirely to me. Living away from home brought a mix of freedom and responsibility. There was no one to remind me to wake up, no one to cook, no one to tell me to study. I had to figure it all out on my own.

I learned how to cook the simplest meals—nothing fancy, but enough to get by. My first few tries weren't great. I burned eggs, overcooked pasta, and once set off the smoke alarm trying to bake chicken. Still, each small mistake taught me something. I learned how to budget the little money I had, how to stretch a grocery trip into two weeks, and how to manage my time between classes, studying, and social life.

Balancing everything didn't come easy. There

were days when I felt overwhelmed, when homesickness crept in late at night and the walls of my dorm room felt too quiet. But there were also days when laughter filled the air—when I'd look around at my roommates and realize that I was building something I had longed for: a sense of belonging.

My roommates came from different parts of the country, each with her own story, accent, and rhythm. We were different, yet connected by the shared adventure of figuring out adulthood together. We stayed up late talking about everything: school, family, love, dreams, and the kind of hopes you only dare to speak about when you're eighteen and the world still feels wide open.

Some nights, we laughed until we cried, huddled together in a tiny dorm room with snacks scattered across the floor. I still remember one night in particular, when we had all finished our first round of exams and the tension finally broke. Someone suggested we tell our "worst first day stories." One by one, we confessed our most embarrassing moments—missed alarms, wrong classrooms, locked dorm doors, and burnt popcorn setting off alarms. We laughed until our sides hurt, until the quiet hours of the night turned into dawn.

Those were the kinds of moments that stitched us together. Even now, years later, we still check in with one another—birthdays, holidays, or just random "thinking of you" messages. The connection we built in those early days of college remains a quiet reminder that even when I was far from home, I was never truly alone.

Music continued to be my anchor. Piano,

dance, and band remained woven into my life, grounding me when everything else felt new and uncertain. During my freshman year, I joined the band again, picking up my clarinet after a long pause. It took a little while to find my rhythm—to remember how to breathe in time with the music and blend into an ensemble that felt so much bigger than myself.

The rehearsals became my therapy. Whenever classes felt too demanding or the noise of college life overwhelmed me, I turned to music. The clarinet's tone—soft and steady—reminded me of home, of long afternoons at the piano when the world used to quiet down just enough for me to think clearly. Music was familiar. It reminded me of the strength that had carried me through every chapter of my life so far.

By the second semester of freshman year, something in me began to shift. I started to feel more confident both physically and emotionally. The right leg that had once been a source of pain and limitation had healed to the point that I no longer thought twice before running across campus or climbing a flight of stairs. I felt strong—not just in body, but in spirit. The same strength that had once helped me endure now encouraged me to step into challenges by choice, not by force.

That's when I decided to try out for the college cheerleading squad.

It was not a decision I made lightly. The thought of standing in front of others—moving, jumping, performing—scared me. My scars, though healed, still made me self-conscious. I worried about what people would see or think. But then I remembered all the times I had pushed through fear before. If I could survive pain, hospitals, and years of rebuilding myself, surely I could handle one audition.

A close friend helped me prepare. We spent hours practicing cheers, counting beats, and perfecting moves in the gym when it was empty. She corrected my form, cheered me on when I grew frustrated, and reminded me, "You've got this."

The day of tryouts, I was a bundle of nerves. The gym echoed with voices, sneakers squeaking against the polished floor, and music playing faintly from someone's speaker. As I stood waiting for my turn I felt that old fear of being seen rise again. But when I stepped forward, everything went quiet inside me. I took a deep breath and remembered all the years of work it took to get here. I gave it my all.

When the results were posted, I hesitated to look. My heart pounded as I scanned the list of names. And there it was. Seeing it written there—bold and certain—was a feeling I'll never forget.

Making the cheerleading team was more than an achievement; it was a personal victory. It was proof that every hardship, every painful memory, every night I spent rebuilding my confidence had led to this moment. I had done something I once thought impossible.

I was no longer just surviving; I was living, thriving, and stepping into the fullness of who I was becoming.

My coach played a significant part in that transformation. She believed in me from the start—even when I doubted myself. She saw my potential before I could see it clearly. Her encouragement and faith in me opened doors I never imagined I could walk through. I will always be grateful for that. She helped me find my own courage.

Sophomore year arrived quietly, without the excitement and anticipation that had filled my first days on campus. What had begun as a journey of self discovery soon revealed a harder truth: independence can feel heavy when old pain resurfaces. The freedom I once cherished began pressing against me like a weight—I went to class, smiled when expected, and tried to keep up appearances—but inside, I was slipping. Some mornings, even the act of getting out of bed felt impossible. The world outside my dorm window seemed to move too quickly while I lay still beneath the covers, staring at the ceiling, trying to summon the will to move.

My grades began to suffer. Meals lost their taste. The laughter that used to come easily with friends felt distant. I told myself it was just exhaustion—that I needed a break—but I knew it was more. The past I had fought so hard to rise above was whispering again, reminding me of wounds I hadn't fully healed.

Eventually, I knew I couldn't keep pretending. I needed help beyond what campus could offer. So, I made the difficult decision to return home to Virginia, leaving behind the familiar hallways and faces of college life. Home felt both comforting and confronting. It was where my story had begun—but it also held the memories of everything I had endured.

My sister, sensing that I needed a change of scenery, invited me to California to stay with her for a while. I remember the flight—the sky outside the window shifting from pale blue to deep orange as the sun set—and how I promised myself somewhere above the clouds that I would try to heal this time. Truly heal.

California was a world away from Virginia's quiet rhythm. The ocean air carried a softness I hadn't known I needed. My sister welcomed me with open arms, her energy calm but steady—the way family love feels when words aren't enough. She cared for me in ways I didn't realize I needed: making sure I ate, encouraging me to walk outside, and listening without judgment when tears came unexpectedly.

Some days we sat on her porch in silence, watching the sky turn pink over the water. Other days, we took long drives with music playing softly between us. Those moments stitched me back together slowly. Her presence reminded me that strength isn't always loud. It can be gentle, patient, and steady. She saw in me what I had forgotten—a woman who had already overcome so much and who was capable of rising again.

With her help, I began rebuilding piece by piece. I started journaling again, revisiting the piano when I could find one, and reaching out to friends I had withdrawn from. Therapy and campus resources became part of my healing after I returned to school, helping me untangle what depression had knotted. Little by little, light returned—first as faint glimmers, then as something steady enough to hold.

By the time junior year arrived, I was no longer the same. I returned to campus with clarity, humility, and compassion for myself.

Life, I realized, didn't always go according to plan, but that didn't mean it was off track.

It was during that year that I met someone who made me feel truly seen. His kindness came easily, his laughter warm and disarming. What began as friendship grew into something deeper—the kind of connection that makes you believe love can heal what pain once broke. He made me feel special, cherished, and understood in ways I hadn't known before.

I leaned heavily on the community I had built—the friends who had been with me through late-night study sessions and laughter-filled dorm talks. With them, I found reassurance that I did not have to face this chapter alone. Their support became my anchor. They checked on me often, walked me to classes, and made sure I ate when stress dulled my appetite.

Through it all, I held onto the things that had always carried me—music, dance, cheer, and band. When uncertainty felt heavy, I returned to rhythm and movement. Piano remained my sanctuary; each note felt like a prayer for strength. Cheering kept my spirit engaged. The squeak of sneakers on polished gym floors, the echo of laughter between teammates, and the quick exchange of encouragement reminded me that joy could exist even in seasons of transition.

Academically, I began to thrive again. My focus returned stronger than before. That year, I made the Dean's List—a personal victory that meant more than any award. It wasn't just about grades; it proved I had survived the darkness of the previous year and emerged stronger.

I still remember one late afternoon practice in the gym. Sunlight spilled through high windows, streaking across the polished floor. The room buzzed with laughter and the rhythmic sounds of drills. We were exhausted—sweat dripping, hair stuck to our faces—but none of that mattered. We pushed through the routine again and again, cheering each other on until it felt perfect. When I finally nailed a difficult sequence I'd struggled with for weeks, my friend—the same one who helped me prepare freshman year—let out a loud whoop. We collapsed in the corner laughing, proud and breathless. In that small, joy-filled moment, something inside me lifted.

Those moments reminded me that triumph doesn't always arrive in grand gestures.

Sometimes it appears quietly—in persistence, in support, in the simple courage to keep showing up even when life shifts beneath you.

My college journey didn't unfold the way I imagined it would, but maybe that was the point. Every twist and detour brought growth I could never have planned. I learned independence—not just in managing time or finances, but in owning my voice. I learned how to ask for help without shame, how to rebuild after setbacks, and how to see beauty in unexpected turns.

College was more than an education; it was a transformation. It taught me that healing isn't linear, that strength can coexist with vulnerability, and that new beginnings often rise out of the hardest seasons.

When I learned I was expecting my first child, the world tilted again—but this time, I didn't crumble. There was fear and uncertainty, yes, but beneath it was a quiet strength that whispered, "You can do this." Motherhood found me sooner than expected, and though the path ahead was unknown, I felt a strange peace in accepting it.

That moment changed everything. It reshaped how I saw myself—not just as a student or survivor, but as a woman stepping into a new kind of purpose. I began to understand love in a way I never had before: as something that requires courage, responsibility, and faith all at once.

By the time I left campus for the last time, I wasn't the same girl who had arrived with wide eyes and nervous hands. I was a woman—wiser, steadier, and ready to step into a life that would soon include new responsibilities and new love.

The strength I had forged through pain and healing became my foundation as I stepped into motherhood. What lay ahead would challenge me in ways I couldn't yet imagine, but I carried with me everything those years had taught me: faith, resilience, and the unwavering belief that I could rise again, no matter how many times life required it.

Motherhood did not erase who I was—it revealed who I had always been becoming.

Chapter 6 — Building a New Life

☼

College had given me independence, confidence, and the strength to face challenges. I carried those lessons with me as life moved beyond campus and into territory I could never have planned.

Change does not always announce itself. Sometimes it arrives quietly, asking you to pause and look more closely. For me, that quiet turning point came when the future I had imagined began to reshape itself—subtle at first, then undeniable.

I remember the moment vividly, not because of where I was, but because of how it felt. My body reacted before my mind could catch up. My hands trembled, my breath felt shallow, and the world around me seemed to shrink. It wasn't panic alone—it was the realization that my life was no longer centered solely on me. Something new was taking shape, and I could feel the weight of that truth settling deep within me.

Learning I was going to become a mother carried both softness and gravity. Fear surfaced, yes, but alongside it was an unexpected calm—as if everything I had endured before had been preparing me for this shift. I moved through my days carefully, holding that knowledge close, letting ordinary moments take on new meaning as I adjusted to what was unfolding.

When I finally found the courage to tell my parents, it felt harder than any challenge I had faced before. My voice shook, my palms were damp, and I felt suspended between who I had been and the life unfolding ahead of me. I braced myself for disappointment, unsure of how this next chapter would be received.

My parents, shaped by tradition and community expectations, encouraged me toward what they believed would provide stability. They spoke about responsibility, about building a home, about giving my child security. Their words came from love, even if I could not fully understand them at the time.

The advice came quickly—too quickly for my overwhelmed heart to process. I nodded through conversations while my thoughts raced. I felt suspended between two versions of myself—the college student still discovering her dreams and the woman about to step into motherhood. The space between those versions felt impossibly wide.

Following their guidance, I married the father of my child and stepped into a new chapter marked by hope and uncertainty. Our wedding was a grand celebration, full of good intentions and expectations. I wore an elegant dress and reminded myself that I was choosing what I believed to be responsible and loving. As I walked down the aisle, excitement mingled with doubt. I hoped commitment would nurture love, even as I stepped into a future I did not yet fully understand.

Our oldest was six months old when we married. By then, the life inside me had become a baby with bright eyes, soft hands, and a presence that changed everything. Each time his fingers wrapped around mine, a new kind of courage surfaced. He anchored me when emotions felt too large to hold.

Soon after, I moved to his hometown, leaving my childhood home behind. Packing was different than I expected. My home held layers of memory—laughter, pain, comfort, and roots. With every box sealed shut, a piece of my old life folded away. The drive felt long, even if it wasn't. Familiar landmarks faded, replaced by roads I did not yet recognize.

The move was more than physical. It was emotional. I was stepping into a life I had not planned, believing that beginnings sometimes look like sacrifice rather than excitement.

Over the next five years, life offered another unexpected blessing: twins—a boy and a girl. Seeing two heartbeats flicker on the ultrasound screen felt surreal. I laughed through shock and wonder, hands instinctively resting on my stomach. The thought of three children under six felt overwhelming, yet beneath the anxiety was a steady warmth—a sense that life was unfolding with purpose, even if I could not yet see it clearly.

The day the twins were born remains vivid. The room buzzed with nurses and monitors, but my focus rested on their tiny faces—one crying softly, the other blinking up at me as if absorbing the world. My oldest watched with wide-eyed curiosity, unsure at first, then captivated.

The early weeks blurred together—bottles, blankets, diapers, late-night feedings stretching into morning. Exhausting, yes, but sacred. Love filled the space even when sleep did not.

Motherhood settled into me like something I had been waiting for without knowing it.

Everything I had survived became a lesson I never wanted my children to learn the hard way. I promised myself I would build a home filled with patience, honesty, and safety—a place where they would always feel seen.

The responsibility did not frighten me. It gave me balance. It gave my life direction.

Balancing school, work, and three young children became a daily test of endurance. Textbooks lay open beside the kitchen counter. Homework happened during nap time. Essays were typed late at night with a baby monitor humming nearby. Some days I felt stretched thin—one child crying, another hungry, another needing comfort all at once. Somehow, I made it work.

Each small milestone became a victory: passing a class, managing the household, getting through a day without feeling completely overwhelmed. These moments were not glamorous, but they were proof of growth happening quietly, inch by inch.

Over time, it became clear that the marriage—entered with care and intention—could not continue in a healthy way. The realization came slowly, through silence and conversations that went nowhere. We were young, growing in different directions, and sometimes growth pulls people apart.

We separated with respect, committed to raising our children with stability and love. It was not a failure, but a transition—one that allowed me to breathe again.

Co-parenting became another lesson in patience and adaptability. I refused to view the experience as a mistake. It was part of my growth—another step forward, not backward.

Motherhood, marriage, separation—none came with instructions. Yet whenever doubt crept in, I remembered the girl I once was: the one who endured pain, survived silence, pushed through depression, and kept moving forward.

She had always been stronger than she realized.

Determination became my companion. Some mornings began in chaos—backpacks by the door, permission slips missing, the rush to get everyone out on time. Strength was not loud. It was choosing to keep going anyway.

Patience came slowly. I learned to give it to my children and to myself. I stopped expecting perfection and allowed growth to happen one day at a time.

I learned to hold both versions of myself—

the mother who gave endlessly and the woman whose dreams still lived quietly. I did not have to choose between them. I could be both.

My strength was no longer something I had to prove. It was steady, honest, and earned.

I worked to create a home where love came first, where mistakes were met with grace, and where resilience was modeled, not demanded. Rebuilding did not happen in one moment. It happened in daily choices—choosing peace, choosing presence, choosing to show up.

Looking back, I can see how every effort—the late nights, early mornings, whispered prayers—was shaping me into someone stronger and more capable.

My life was not easy, but it was mine. Without realizing it, I had been laying a foundation all along.

I was no longer reacting to life as it happened. I was building something—intentionally, imperfectly, and with care.

And in the quiet work of each ordinary day, I learned that building a new life doesn't happen in triumph—it happens in the courage to keep going.

Keeping going required more than endurance; it required intention. I had to learn how to listen to myself again—to the quiet signals of exhaustion, to the moments when I needed help, to the truth beneath the roles I was fulfilling. Motherhood had taught me how to pour out; this season was teaching me how to refill. I was beginning to understand that strength without rest eventually turns into depletion.

There were days when the weight of responsibility pressed hard against my chest. Decisions felt heavier now because they reached beyond me, shaping the lives of three small people who trusted me completely. Yet within that weight, there was clarity. I knew what mattered. I knew what I was willing to fight for. The chaos of earlier years had sharpened my sense of priority.

I also began to recognize the quiet grief woven into new beginnings—the mourning of paths not taken, versions of life I once imagined. Letting go did not come easily. But I learned that release does not erase meaning; it makes room. Every ending carried the seed of something honest and necessary.

In the stillness after long days, I sometimes sat alone and felt the layers of my life settling into place. I was no longer the girl trying to be chosen or corrected. I was no longer defined by survival alone. I was becoming a woman shaped by choice, responsibility, and resolve.

What I did not yet know was that building stability would awaken questions I had long avoided—about identity, faith, worth, and the cost of carrying everything alone. Strength had brought me this far, but the next season would ask me to examine it more closely.

Because eventually, building a life is not just about what you can withstand—it is about what you are willing to confront.

The quiet mattered more than I expected. After the children were asleep and the house finally settled, I would sit alone and feel the day sink into my body. Some nights I was tired down to my bones. Other nights my mind stayed busy, replaying choices I had made and wondering if I was getting it right. I didn't search for answers. I just listened.

I began to notice how often I put myself last, not because anyone asked me to, but because it had become normal. Caring for others had taught me how to keep going, how to push through, how to ignore discomfort. Learning to pause felt unfamiliar. Rest did not come easily. Stillness made room for thoughts I wasn't used to hearing.

There were parts of myself I had set aside without realizing it—interests, dreams, small desires that didn't fit neatly into the life I was building. I didn't reach for them all at once. I simply acknowledged they were still there. That recognition felt important.

I also became more aware of what I wanted to cultivate in my home. Peace mattered. Stability mattered. The tone of everyday life mattered. I paid attention to how my children responded to routine, to consistency, to the simple comfort of knowing what came next. I wanted them to grow up feeling secure, surrounded by steadiness and care.

The days continued to be full. School schedules, work hours, grocery lists, bedtime routines—nothing slowed down. But inside me, something was shifting. I was no longer just reacting to what life placed in front of me. I was thinking ahead. Choosing carefully. Learning when to say yes and when to step back.

I didn't have everything figured out. I still doubted myself. I still felt stretched thin. But I trusted myself more than I used to. I trusted that I could handle what came next, even if I couldn't see it yet.

The life I was building felt steady on the outside. On the inside, it was preparing me for changes I hadn't named yet—changes that would ask me to look at my life, my choices, and myself in new ways.

And slowly, without any grand moment or clear beginning, the next season started to unfold.

Rebuilding is not starting over. It is carrying what you survived and choosing how it shapes you.

Chapter 7 — Rebuilding and Thriving

☼

Separating from my marriage brought its own emotions, and in that space, I focused on what I could control—my choices and my actions. The emotions were unpredictable, sweeping over me in waves. One moment I felt relief; the next, the weight of what I had lost. Some days felt light, filled with clarity and resolve. Other days felt heavy, as if grief had settled quietly into my chest without warning. But in the midst of that upheaval, I realized there was one thing I could always rely on: my ability to choose.

I could decide how to respond to the

situation, how to carry myself, and how to shape the journey ahead. This realization didn't erase the pain of separation, but it offered a sense of agency at a time when everything else felt uncertain. It was a quiet but powerful shift, choosing to anchor myself in what I could control instead of dwelling on what was gone. That choice became my compass.

Though my divorce was still in process, my heart had already moved forward. The separation itself had become a closed chapter long before the paperwork caught up. Emotionally, I had done the work of letting go—grieving what was and releasing what could no longer be. In every way that mattered, the marriage was already behind me.

As time passed, I watched my children —now older, now stretching into their own identities— adjust to our new reality. Two were in middle school, and one was in high school. Their independence was growing, but so were their needs for structure, guidance, and consistency. Watching them mature, I understood that while they were becoming more autonomous, they still needed a foundation of stability to thrive. Adolescence brought questions, challenges, and moments when they tested boundaries as they searched for themselves.

My role, though evolving, remained the same: to be their constant. The balance between giving them space to grow and ensuring they felt secure was delicate. Some days required firm guidance; others called for listening and patience. The more they changed, the more I needed to remain steady—the safe place they could always return to. I wanted them to know that no matter how life shifted, home was still solid.

While my children's independence expanded, my own sense of stability was anchored in my work. I continued teaching, a career built with dedication and love. Teaching was never just a job; it was my calling. The classroom became my second home, a place where I felt purposeful and assured. It wasn't simply the curriculum or daily routines—it was the environment of growth, the relationships, the connections, the spark in a young person's eyes when something finally made sense.

Stepping into the classroom reminded me of who I was before everything shifted: a passionate educator devoted to inspiring and guiding others. It was the constant that kept me steady amidst the turbulence of change. Each day I showed up for my students, I was also showing up for myself.

Teaching wasn't something I found after the transition; it was what carried me through it. It wasn't an escape — it was a lifeline. In the midst of emotional unraveling, the rhythm of the classroom offered normalcy. The energy of learning brought a joy that was difficult to find anywhere else. Each lesson I prepared refocused me on something greater than myself, and in doing so, it began to heal me. My work wasn't a distraction; it was the one thing that remained clear and dependable when everything else felt uncertain.

But rebuilding required more than commitment to work. I soon realized I needed to nurture myself mentally, physically, and emotionally. At first, this felt optional — something to postpone. There was always something else demanding my attention. But as I continued forward, I understood that self-care wasn't indulgent; it was essential. Without it, I would eventually run dry.

Waking up early for a quiet walk, journaling before dawn, sitting with a cup of coffee in silence, pausing to breathe deeply during moments of overwhelm—these small choices became tools for restoration. They steadied me when emotions ran high and reminded me that I deserved care too. Self-care became a cornerstone of my healing, not because it solved everything, but because it helped me stay present.

Even through exhaustion and setbacks, I found reasons to celebrate. Each achievement my children reached, every school event, every personal milestone reminded me how far we had come. It was easy to focus on what wasn't working, but when I stepped back, I saw progress — theirs and mine. Each small victory felt like a triumph, proof that even through challenges, we were adapting, growing, and moving forward. Those moments, however small, reminded me that despite everything we had endured, life still held joy.

All three of my children graduated high school and went on to college — a milestone I had imagined for years. Watching them cross those stages filled me with awe. I remembered the days when just getting through a morning felt overwhelming, and now here they were, stepping confidently into their futures.

My oldest earned his bachelor's degree and continued into graduate school, his determination shining brighter than ever. My twins, now juniors in college, were carving their own paths with confidence, each blossoming into their own identity.

Witnessing their strength and independence affirmed what perseverance and love can build. Seeing it reflected in their lives reminded me how far we had all come. Their successes didn't just make me proud of them — they made me proud of the woman I had become walking beside them.

Through all of this, I came to understand that rebuilding wasn't about starting over. It was about stepping forward — taking the lessons of the past, the heartaches, struggles, and triumphs, and transforming them into wisdom and clarity. For years, I had focused on what I had been through—the chapters behind me. But as I watched my children rise, I realized rebuilding wasn't about erasing the past. It was about honoring it, integrating it, and letting it propel me forward.

I was no longer the young mother uncertain

of her future. I had become a woman shaped in resilience, stepping into the next chapter with intention. I understood now that strength isn't about being unbreakable — it's about rising every time you fall. The woman I had become didn't look back with regret. She embraced her scars and used them as tools.

And as life continued to unfold, I began to understand another truth: we don't rebuild alone. We rebuild with support, connection, and the people brave enough to walk beside us. I didn't yet know how deeply that truth would shape my next season of life — the season where sister-friends would not only support me, but help carry me. I didn't yet realize how vital that truth would become, or how profoundly it would shape the next chapter of my story — the chapter where sister-friends would become family, and healing would take on a new and powerful form.

At that point in my life, connection began to feel different than it once had. I no longer reached for people out of fear of being alone or a need to be rescued. I was learning to choose companionship from a place of wholeness, not lack. I paid attention to how people made me feel after conversations—whether I felt lighter or more burdened, understood or diminished. Discernment, once learned through hardship, had become one of my quiet strengths.

I noticed how healing unfolded not in grand gestures, but in shared moments: conversations that lingered longer than expected, laughter that came easily, silence that felt safe instead of awkward. There was comfort in knowing I didn't have to explain everything to be understood. Some people simply met me where I was, without judgment or expectation. That kind of presence felt rare—and precious.

As my children grew more independent, space opened in my life in unfamiliar ways. The house was quieter. My responsibilities shifted. For the first time in years, I had room to consider myself not only as a mother or provider, but as a woman with her own needs, interests, and capacity for joy. That space felt both freeing and intimidating. Growth often does.

I began saying yes to things that once felt unnecessary—coffee with a friend, a walk after work, moments of rest without justification. These were not escapes from responsibility; they were invitations back to myself. I was learning that rebuilding also meant allowing joy to return, even after long seasons of survival.

There was a deep comfort in realizing I no longer needed to perform strength. I could be honest about tiredness. I could admit uncertainty. I could ask for help without feeling diminished by it. The version of strength I now carried was quieter, steadier, and far more sustainable than anything I had known before.

Looking back, I can see that this season wasn't about dramatic change, but about alignment. My life began to feel more like my own—guided by intention rather than reaction. I trusted myself in ways I hadn't before. I trusted the pace. I trusted the process. And I trusted that what was forming around me was not accidental.

I didn't yet have language for what was coming next, only a sense that I was no longer meant to walk alone. The foundation had been laid—through loss, growth, motherhood, and resilience—for relationships that would nurture rather than drain me. The kind of bonds that don't just witness your healing, but participate in it.

Rebuilding had given me stability. Thriving was teaching me connection.

And quietly, without fanfare, the circle around me began to grow.

I learned that chosen family can hold you just as tightly—and sometimes more gently—than blood ever could.

Chapter 8 — Sister-Friends: Finding My Circle

☼

During this period of my life, I met two extraordinary women who would become my sister-friends. I quickly learned that true friendship isn't defined by how long you've known someone, but by who shows up—consistently, lovingly, and without hesitation—in the moments that matter most. These women showed up in ways that transformed my life.

The bonds I formed with them were far more than casual friendships. They were anchoring, healing, and essential to my survival. They helped me navigate motherhood, career-building, and the emotional work of rediscovering myself. They were my laughter, my refuge, and my safe spaces—relationships that stood firm as life's twists and turns grew more unpredictable.

For much of my life, I believed strength meant independence. Carrying everything alone felt like the only way forward. Through their steady presence, that belief began to shift. I learned that strength could also look like trust—allowing myself to lean on others without guilt or apology. With them, I discovered a truth I hadn't known how to accept before: leaning on others does not weaken you; it sustains you.

They showed up in quiet, meaningful ways. They called on days when exhaustion weighed heavy. They dropped off dinner when cooking felt impossible. Their care was never dramatic—just steady, reliable, and full of intention. We shared laughter that left our stomachs aching and conversations that uncovered fears, doubts, and hopes we rarely voiced aloud. Those honest moments became the foundation of our bond.

I treasure the countless hours we spent together—long conversations over coffee, quiet walks to clear our minds, spontaneous road trips without agendas. Their friendship taught me the importance of pausing, of giving myself permission to rest and breathe. They reminded me that caring for myself was not selfish—it was necessary.

They celebrated my victories as if they were their own and stood beside me through setbacks with unwavering loyalty. Their presence reinforced what I had long forgotten: support is not a luxury; it is a necessity. At the time, I did not yet realize how vital that foundation would become—but the strength they helped me build would soon be tested in ways I could not have anticipated.

I spent years believing strength meant carrying everything alone. Healing taught me that strength also means knowing when to lean.

Chapter 9 — The Power of Friendship: Learning to Lean

☼

The bonds I shared with my sister-friends became a constant presence in my life—steadfast, grounding, and unshakable. Their love, guidance, and belief in me carried me through both the ordinary demands of daily life and the moments that tested my resilience most deeply.

What I came to understand through these relationships was the power of consistency. True support is not loud—it is reliable. It is knowing someone will answer when you call, sit beside you without needing explanations, and remain present when life grows heavy. With the right people beside you, even the hardest moments feel survivable.

Their presence allowed me to be honest in ways I had not permitted myself before. I no longer felt the need to minimize my struggles or package my pain so it would be easier for others to receive. I could speak openly about exhaustion, uncertainty, and fear without being met with judgment. Being fully seen did not make me feel exposed—it made me feel safe.

I learned that real connection is built where vulnerability and trust meet. These friendships were not rooted in obligation or convenience, but in care and intention. They did not disappear during difficult seasons. They remained steady and present when it mattered most.

There were seasons when responsibility felt relentless. Motherhood, work, and personal growth often demanded more than I felt capable of giving. In those moments, friendship became a stabilizing force. I was reminded that I did not need to have everything figured out to keep moving forward, and that it was okay to pause when the weight became too heavy.

Through these relationships, I came to understand that love and loyalty are lifelines. True friendship lifts you when life feels heavy and helps you rise when you feel like falling. These connections did more than help me endure life's challenges—they strengthened me for what was still ahead.

Grief does not weaken love. It proves how deeply love once lived.

Chapter 10 — Strength in the Midst of Loss

☼

The loss of my mother in 2021 brought a grief unlike anything I had ever known. Even after years spent rebuilding my life, nothing prepared me for the weight of her absence. Her love was woven into every part of who I was; losing her felt as though the center of my world had shifted.

In the days following her passing, I moved through life in a haze. I showed up because that was what I knew how to do. There were children who still needed me and responsibilities that could not wait. I kept moving, believing that staying busy was the same as coping.

I learned quickly that grief does not follow a schedule. It arrives in waves—sometimes gentle, sometimes overwhelming. I mourned not only the woman I lost, but the unrealized moments and the quiet comfort of her presence. Grief appeared without warning: a familiar song, a phrase spoken in her voice, a memory that settled deep in my chest.

Even in my sorrow, I held tightly to the lessons my mother had instilled in me—resilience, perseverance, and the importance of showing up. Honoring her legacy meant continuing to be the mother my children needed.

Loving them through my grief became a quiet act of devotion.

During this season, my children, along with sister-friends and steady siblings, became more than a support system—they became my lifeline. They reminded me that strength is not measured by suffering alone, but by allowing others to hold space for you when you cannot hold everything yourself.

Grief taught me that healing does not mean forgetting. It means learning how to carry love and loss side by side, allowing joy to exist without guilt and sadness to exist without shame. Over time, glimmers of hope returned. My mother's legacy lives on in the relationships I nurture and the life I continue to build.

Loss does not end the story. It asks you to decide what you will carry forward—and what you will finally lay down.

Chapter 11 — Carrying Loss, Choosing Strength

☼

After my mother's passing, life's challenges deepened in ways I did not expect. Grief settled into my days as a constant companion. Her absence created a silence that lingered, making everything feel fragile.

As I tried to steady myself, family dynamics began to fracture. Some of my siblings, overwhelmed by their own struggles with addiction, drifted further away. The distance revealed emotional gaps I had hoped time and love might heal. Accepting that not every relationship survives shared loss was painful, but necessary for my own well-being.

Learning to release those expectations became another form of grief. I realized that choosing self-preservation did not mean abandoning those I loved—it meant acknowledging what I could and could not carry. Boundaries were not walls; they were protections that allowed love to remain honest and sustainable.

During this time, my children became my foundation. They were navigating early adulthood—and their resilience reminded me daily that I still had purpose. Even in my weakest moments, they unknowingly held me steady.

In 2024, grief returned with the passing of my father. This loss carried a different weight—a deep exhaustion that reopened wounds I believed had begun to heal. Once again, family dynamics shifted. I learned that grief is deeply personal, and I could not control how anyone else moved through it. I could only choose my own way forward.

Through these compounded losses, I uncovered a deeper understanding of resilience. Guided by the steady support of my children and the people who remained close, I learned that strength is not about enduring endlessly—it is about knowing when to lean, when to rest, and when to ask for help.

Peace did not come from forgetting what I survived. It came from learning how to live fully beside it.

Chapter 12 — Moving Forward: Finding Peace, Purpose, and Love

☼

Looking back, I can see how every challenge—from childhood wounds to the heartbreaks of adulthood and the profound losses of my parents—shaped the woman I am today. The clarity I once fought to reclaim settled into a quiet acceptance that life is a continuous process of breaking, becoming, and rebuilding.

The journey through grief taught me that healing does not mean forgetting, nor does it grant immunity from future pain. It means learning how to carry love and loss side by side, allowing joy to exist without guilt and sadness to exist without shame.

I learned that resilience is not about standing alone, but about knowing when to lean on the pillars in my life—my children, my friends, and the people who chose to stay. They taught me that true strength is not the absence of vulnerability, but the courage to move forward anyway.

Ultimately, I discovered that my purpose lies in integration. The moments of sorrow became teachers, revealing that I could honor pain while still welcoming joy. Anchored by my children and strengthened by love, I step forward into a new season—not untouched by loss, but rooted in peace and purpose.

Epilogue

I have learned that pain does not define me. It shaped me, yes—but it did not win.

I am still standing. Still growing. Still healing. And most importantly, still rebuilding.

There was a time when survival demanded everything I had. I learned how to function without rest, how to push through emotional pain without naming it, how to stay strong even when strength felt isolating. Endurance became instinct. Silence became habit. And moving forward—no matter the cost—felt like the only option.

But survival was never meant to be the end of the story.

Over time, I learned that strength does not require self-erasure. Healing does not require forgetting. And faith does not ask us to deny pain—it invites us to walk through it with honesty. What once felt like weakness revealed itself as resilience shaped through fire.

I no longer measure my life by what I survived, but by how fully I am able to live now. The urgency that once governed my choices has softened into intention. I move more slowly, more deliberately, with an awareness that healing is not a destination but a practice—one I return to daily, remembering that peace is something I am allowed to have.

There are still days when memories rise without warning, when grief or doubt taps quietly at the door of my thoughts. But they no longer control me. I have learned how to sit with discomfort without surrendering to it, how to honor what shaped me without allowing it to define every step forward. Faith continues to steady me, motherhood continues to ground me, and becoming remains an unfolding process rather than a finished state.

What remains is not perfection, but presence. Not certainty, but trust. And not a life untouched by pain—but a life rooted in truth, love, and the courage to continue.

"I can do all things through Christ who strengthens me."
— Philippians 4:13

This memoir is my testimony—a testament to resilience, faith, and the unwavering truth that even in the darkest moments, there is light. Even in brokenness, there is beauty. And even in life's storms, there is strength waiting to rise.

Afterword

For a long time, I believed that surviving was the same thing as living. I did what needed to be done, made the choices that felt necessary at the time, and kept moving forward because stopping never felt like an option. From the outside, that kind of endurance can look like strength. From the inside, it often feels like holding your breath for years at a time—waiting for the moment when it might finally be safe to exhale.

Where I am now is quieter than the life you have just read about. Not easier. Not perfect. But steadier. The urgency that once shaped every decision has softened. I no longer live in constant reaction to what might happen next. Instead, I live in the space between what was and what is still becoming. There are days when I feel secure in who I am, and days when old fears resurface without warning. Healing did not arrive all at once. It arrived in pieces—through awareness, boundaries, grief, and the slow permission to rest. It arrived through small moments that would have once seemed insignificant: a deep breath taken without force, a decision made without panic, an evening that ended without the familiar knot of dread. It arrived through repetition—through choosing myself, not once, but over and over, until that choice began to feel less like rebellion and more like responsibility.

Motherhood looks different to me now than it did when I was simply trying to survive it. I understand my children differently, and I understand myself differently. I see now how much of my early parenting was shaped by fear—fear of repeating cycles, fear of failing them, fear of not being enough. I believed that vigilance was love, that exhaustion was proof of devotion. I did the best I could with what I knew then. What I am learning now is how to extend the same compassion to myself that I so easily offer to others. I am learning that my children do not need a mother who is constantly depleted in order to feel cared for. They need a mother who is present—someone who can listen without rushing, respond without exploding, and rest without apologizing. I am learning that tenderness is not a luxury in parenting; it is a foundation. And I am learning that the way I speak to myself becomes the atmosphere my children grow in, even when I think they are not paying attention.

Survival came at a cost. It required me to silence parts of myself that felt inconvenient or too vulnerable to carry while everything else demanded my attention. What I didn't understand at the time was how much of myself I was postponing—how many feelings I stored away for "later," when life finally slowed down enough to feel safe. Only with distance could I see that many of the choices I once judged myself for were acts of preservation. Some of those choices were not pretty. Some of them were complicated. Some of them hurt people, including me. But I can see now how fear narrows the available options, how the mind chooses what it believes will keep the body intact. I can see now that I wasn't choosing from freedom—I was choosing from scarcity, from pressure, from the constant need to adapt. That realization does not excuse everything, but it gives context, and context makes compassion possible.

Exhaustion was evidence of how much I was holding. Struggle did not mean weakness; it meant I was still trying. Questioning myself was not failure—it was the beginning of awareness. These realizations did not erase the past, but they reframed it. They allowed me to see my younger self with tenderness instead of judgment, and to honor the ways she protected me when no one else could. I can look back now and recognize how hard she worked to make it through each day, how she learned to anticipate needs before they were spoken, how she learned to be small when it seemed safer to disappear, how she learned to be loud when silence was mistaken for consent. I can recognize that she did not have the language for what she was experiencing, but she had instincts, and those instincts kept me alive. The older I get, the more I understand that survival is not always heroic in the way stories make it sound. Sometimes it is just relentless. Sometimes it is quiet. Sometimes it is waking up and doing it again.

Grief still exists in my life, but it no longer defines it. Loss changed me in ways I will always carry, but it also clarified what matters. Grief taught me that love does not disappear when someone does—it changes shape. It becomes memory, influence, and presence in quieter forms. I no longer rush myself through grief or try to outrun it. Some days it is heavier than others, and I allow that to be true. Healing did not require me to forget; it required me to integrate. Integration has meant learning how to live with what happened without letting it become the only lens through which I see myself. It has meant accepting that some pain does not end—it evolves. It becomes something I learn to hold differently. It becomes something I carry with more skill, more honesty, more softness. I have learned that grief is not a sign that healing failed; it is a sign that something mattered. And it is possible, even now, to feel joy without betraying what I lost.

One of the hardest lessons I learned was that breaking cycles often means disappointing people who benefited from your silence. Setting boundaries came with guilt and doubt. It meant accepting that not everyone would understand my choices—and that understanding was not required for me to move forward. Motherhood demanded that I become someone who could say no, even when my voice shook. It demanded that I choose peace over familiarity and honesty over comfort. It demanded that I trust myself, even when that trust felt fragile. It demanded that I stop negotiating with the parts of me that were trained to keep the peace at my own expense. Breaking cycles required me to accept a new kind of discomfort—the discomfort of being misunderstood, the discomfort of not being liked, the discomfort of recognizing that some relationships only functioned when I stayed small. I had to learn that guilt is not always a warning sign. Sometimes guilt is simply the residue of old conditioning. Sometimes it is what shows up when you begin to choose yourself after years of choosing everyone else.

I no longer confuse endurance with worth. I no longer believe that suffering is a prerequisite for love or belonging. I am learning how to rest without guilt, how to trust quiet moments, how to believe that stability is something I am allowed to have. This has been one of the hardest shifts of all—to accept that life does not need to be earned through constant sacrifice. Rest, for me, has not been a simple act. It has been a practice. It has been relearning how to sit down without scanning for danger, how to enjoy without bracing for consequence, how to stop performing strength long enough to feel what I actually need. There were times when calm felt unfamiliar, even suspicious, as if something must be wrong if everything was quiet. But slowly, I have begun to understand that peace is not something that arrives all at once. Peace is built. It is maintained. It is chosen in the smallest ways—through boundaries, through honesty, through saying no, through leaving what is unhealthy, through staying with myself.

If you are reading this and recognize yourself in any part of this story, I want you to know something important: survival is not something to minimize. If you did what you had to do to get through, that does not make you broken—it makes you human. Healing does not mean erasing the past or pretending it didn't hurt. It means learning how to live alongside what shaped you without allowing it to dictate everything you are permitted to become. It means understanding that survival strategies often outlive the danger that created them, and learning—slowly, imperfectly—how to put them down. It means learning that you can be both strong and tired, both capable and in need, both grateful to be here and honest about what it cost to get here. It means allowing yourself to be a whole person again, not just a functioning one.

I am still rebuilding. I am still learning. This book is not a declaration that everything has been resolved. It is an acknowledgment that I survived, that I grew, and that I continue to choose a life that feels honest—even when it is uncomfortable, even when it is incomplete. My journey—uneven, unfinished, and complicated—is still worthy of being honored. Becoming does not look like arriving at a final version of myself. It looks like returning to myself. It looks like noticing when I am slipping back into old patterns and reaching for something healthier instead. It looks like choosing repair over shame. It looks like allowing my life to be a work in progress without treating that progress as a deficiency. It looks like accepting that I can be proud of who I am while still wanting to grow.

I am not behind. I am not late to my life. I am not failing because I am still healing. I am learning to release the timeline I once clung to—the one that said I should be "over it" by now, stronger by now, less affected by now. I am learning that healing does not follow a calendar, and that the person I am becoming is not delayed simply because she is taking her time. I am learning that it is possible to move forward without rushing, to build something stable without abandoning myself to do it. I am learning that progress can be quiet, and still real.

I am not behind. I am here—aware, imperfect, and still choosing. Still choosing to tell the truth. Still choosing to rest when I can. Still choosing to love my children without losing myself. Still choosing to believe that stability is not something I must justify. Still choosing to breathe, even when old parts of me want to hold my breath out of habit.

I am not behind. And I do not need to prove anything to be worthy of the life I am building.

Letter to the Reader

If you are holding this book, I want to begin by acknowledging you. Not as an audience, not as a consumer of a story, but as a person who chose to sit with someone else's truth. That choice matters more than it may seem.

This book was not written to instruct or persuade. It was written to name an experience that is often carried quietly—misunderstood, minimized, or mistaken for personal weakness rather than adaptive strength. If you recognized yourself anywhere in these pages—whether in the exhaustion, the vigilance, the grief, or the longing for something steadier—I want you to know that recognition is not accidental. Stories find us when we are ready to see ourselves more clearly.

You may read this book quickly or slowly. You may put it down and come back to it later. You may skip parts that feel too close or linger on sections that give language to something you have never fully named. All of that is allowed. There is no right way to move through this story, just as there is no single path through healing.

If you are someone who has spent years surviving—meeting expectations, managing crises, holding everything together—this book is not asking you to do more. It is not asking you to fix yourself or arrive at some final version of who you should be. It is simply offering companionship in the space between endurance and becoming. It is offering the reminder that survival was never a failure of imagination or effort. It was a response to circumstance.

You may notice that this book does not tie every thread neatly. Some questions remain open. Some relationships are left unresolved. That is intentional. Real lives rarely offer clean conclusions, and healing is not a performance with a finish line. What matters is not whether everything has been repaired, but whether you are learning how to live with greater honesty, agency, and care.

If parts of this book stirred discomfort, I invite you to sit with that gently. Discomfort is often a signal—not of danger, but of truth brushing against something tender. And if parts of this book brought relief, clarity, or a sense of being less alone, I hope you allow yourself to receive that without minimizing it.

You do not need to earn rest.
You do not need to justify your boundaries.
You do not need to suffer in order to belong.

Wherever you are in your own process, I hope this book reminds you that your pace is valid, your experience matters, and your becoming is not behind schedule. You are allowed to build a life that feels sustainable, not just impressive. You are allowed to choose steadiness over struggle. You are allowed to breathe. Thank you for being here.

Reflections

On Survival

Survival is often misunderstood as strength alone. In reality, it is adaptation. It is the body and mind doing whatever is necessary to remain intact under pressure.

Survival narrows our focus. It prioritizes urgency, responsiveness, and endurance. While these skills can be lifesaving, they can also become limiting when the danger has passed but the habits remain. Learning to live after survival requires a different kind of courage—the courage to soften, to slow down, and to trust that safety does not need to be proven every day.

On Living

Living asks for presence instead of vigilance. It asks us to stay when there is nothing to fix, to tolerate calm without waiting for it to collapse, and to allow joy without bracing for loss. For many survivors, living feels unfamiliar at first. It can feel undeserved, even suspicious. But living is not a reward for suffering. It is a right.

On Boundaries

Boundaries are not walls. They are points of clarity. They tell us where responsibility ends and choice begins. Setting boundaries often brings discomfort, especially for those who learned early that love required compliance or silence. But boundaries are how we create space for honesty. They are how we protect what matters without abandoning ourselves in the process.

On Motherhood

Motherhood does not require martyrdom. It requires presence, repair, and growth. Children do not need perfection; they need safety and authenticity. When a parent chooses healing, they are not only changing their own life—they are altering what becomes possible for the next generation. Modeling rest, boundaries, and self-respect teaches lessons that words alone cannot.

On Grief

Grief does not end. It changes. It becomes quieter, less consuming, but no less meaningful. Grief is evidence of love, not a failure to move on. Integrating grief means allowing it to exist without letting it define every moment. It means carrying loss with tenderness instead of resistance.

On Rest

Rest is not inactivity. It is restoration. For those who survived by staying alert, rest can feel unsafe at first. It can trigger guilt or fear. But rest is where integration happens. It is where the nervous system learns that it does not have to be on guard all the time. Rest is a practice, and like all practices, it takes patience.

On Rebuilding

Rebuilding is not linear. It does not move according to deadlines or expectations. It unfolds through awareness, choice, and repetition. Becoming asks us to return to ourselves again and again—to notice what no longer fits, to release what was necessary once but is no longer needed, and to trust that growth can be quiet and still real.

On Worth

Worth is not earned through endurance. It is not proven through exhaustion or sacrifice.

Worth exists because you do. Learning to live from that truth is often the most difficult work of all—and the most freeing.

On Identity

For a long time, my identity was shaped by what I could endure. I learned early that survival required composure. After the burns, the surgeries, the endless appointments where my body was measured, stretched, and altered, I became practiced at tolerating discomfort without complaint. My skin bore evidence of what had happened to me, but my demeanor was expected to be calm, cooperative, grateful. I learned how to be steady long before I understood what it meant to be safe.

Later, when my body was violated in a way I did not yet have language for, that same endurance hardened into armor. I became capable, reliable, unflinching. I learned how to function while dissociating from parts of myself that felt too tender, too exposed. These traits were praised. They were useful. They made me appear strong. But they were never the full story of who I was.

When survival stopped being the organizing force of my life, I felt disoriented. There was no immediate crisis, no medical emergency, no threat requiring vigilance. And in that quiet, a question surfaced that felt more unsettling than pain: *Who am I when my body is no longer something to defend, explain, or endure?*

Reclaiming identity after trauma has not been about reinvention. It has been about remembering. About noticing what remains when I am not defined by scars, by resilience, or by what I have lived through. For years, my sense of self was tethered to usefulness—to how well I managed, how little I asked for, how much I could carry without breaking. Letting go of that identity has felt like losing a language I once depended on to survive.

This process has been slow and, at times, deeply unsettling. There are moments when my body still remembers before my mind does—when tightness, vigilance, or silence rise without warning. But what has begun to emerge beneath those reflexes is something steadier: a sense of self that does not require pain to justify its existence. One that does not need endurance to prove worth.

I am learning that identity is not forged only in trauma. It is revealed in safety. It is uncovered in the moments when I no longer have to brace myself against the world. And perhaps for the first time, I am allowing myself to meet who I am without the need to survive her.

On Forgiveness

Forgiveness is often confused with reconciliation or absolution. For me, it has been neither. Forgiveness has not meant restoring access or minimizing harm. It has meant releasing myself from the work of carrying resentment as evidence of what happened. It has meant choosing not to let the past continue to demand my energy.

Some experiences do not require forgiveness in order to heal. Some wounds are better met with clarity, distance, and acceptance. Forgiveness, when it comes, is not an obligation—it is an option. And it only matters when it serves the person doing the forgiving.

I have learned that I can forgive without forgetting and without reopening doors that were closed for good reason. I can forgive while still honoring boundaries. In this way, forgiveness becomes less about others and more about deciding what I no longer want to carry forward.

On Control

Control can feel like stability when life has been unpredictable. It can masquerade as preparedness, responsibility, or strength. For a long time, I believed that staying in control was how I protected myself and the people I loved. What I did not realize was how much vigilance that belief required—and how little space it left for trust.

Letting go of control has not been a single decision, but a series of small releases. Allowing plans to change. Allowing others to respond in their own way. Allowing myself to rest without scanning for consequences. Each release felt risky, even when nothing was at stake.

What I am learning is that control is not the same as agency. Agency allows for choice, flexibility, and response. Control demands certainty that life cannot offer. Loosening my grip has given me something control never did: room to breathe.

On Hope

Hope does not always arrive as confidence or certainty. Sometimes it shows up quietly, disguised as willingness—a willingness to try again, to imagine something different, to believe that change does not have to be dramatic to be meaningful.

For a long time, hope felt naive to me, something reserved for people whose lives had been less complicated. But I have come to understand that hope is not denial. It is not optimism without evidence. It is the decision to stay open, even when outcomes are unknown.

The hope I carry now is modest and tempered. It does not promise ease or resolution. It promises movement. It promises that becoming is still possible, even here. Even now. And that is enough.

On Continuation

Endings are often imagined as moments of clarity or closure, but most lives do not resolve that way. They continue. They unfold quietly, shaped by small choices rather than definitive conclusions. What matters is not whether everything has been settled, but whether we are willing to stay present as life keeps moving.

Continuation allows for uncertainty without urgency. It allows us to live without demanding guarantees from ourselves or others. It invites patience, not because everything will make sense eventually, but because meaning can exist even while questions remain.

This story does not end with arrival. It ends with intention—with the choice to remain engaged, honest, and open to what comes next. That choice, made again and again, is enough.

Acknowledgments

To my children—thank you for being my heart, my joy, and my greatest inspiration. From the moment you entered my life, you reshaped the way I understood love, purpose, and responsibility. Your curiosity, laughter, and honesty have illuminated my life in ways I never imagined possible. Watching you grow, meet challenges, ask questions, and slowly carve your own paths has shown me what it truly means to be alive.

Every decision I made and every step I took was influenced by my desire to protect you, guide you, and give you something steadier than what I knew. Even in moments when I doubted myself, you gave my life direction. You taught me patience when I wanted answers, resilience when I felt depleted, and the depth of unconditional love simply by being yourselves. You continue to inspire me—not because you ask me to be more, but because you remind me who I already am.

To my sister-friends—the women who became family by choice—thank you for your steadfast presence through every season of my life. Your love, guidance, laughter, and unwavering support carried me through moments when my strength faltered and celebrated me when I could not yet see myself clearly. You taught me the power of connection, loyalty, and showing up without conditions.

You stood beside me in ways both loud and quiet—through late—night conversations, shared silence, encouragement when I felt unsure, and laughter when I needed light. You reminded me that being witnessed without judgment is healing, and that chosen family can be just as grounding as blood. I am endlessly grateful for the strength, wisdom, and light you bring into my life.

To the siblings who remained steady—thank you for showing up with love, support, and understanding when I needed it most. Your presence reminded me that family is not defined by perfection, but by the willingness to stand together through life's storms. I am deeply grateful for those of you who offered consistency, compassion, and connection along the way. Your support mattered more than words can express.

To my dear friends—those who showed up, supported me, laughed with me, and held space through every season—thank you. Your love, loyalty, and presence have been invaluable gifts. You reminded me that authentic connection has the power to transform us, and that friendship does not require perfection—only honesty and care.

To the person who brought new light into my life—thank you for your presence, your steadiness, and the quiet chivalry you have shown during this unfolding chapter. Your support and care reminded me that life still holds beauty, possibility, and connection, even after hardship. You entered my life not to fix what was broken, but to walk beside me as I continued rebuilding. That mattered.

And finally, to my younger self—thank you for surviving. Thank you for holding on, adapting, and rising again and again when the weight felt unbearable. You carried more than you should have, and you did it with courage, instinct, and determination. Your resilience is the heartbeat of this story, and your strength carried me to a place where healing could begin. I honor what you endured, and I release you from the responsibility of carrying what no longer belongs to you.

This book exists because of all of you—because of the love that held me, the connections that shaped me, and the survival that made becoming possible.

About the Author

Kimberly Miller Wynne is a mother, educator, and author whose life and work are grounded in resilience, healing, and intentional living. With over two decades dedicated to education and teaching, she has committed her life's work to supporting growth, reflection, and meaningful connection.

Her years of dedication as an educator have profoundly shaped her voice as a writer. Through careful listening, guidance, and lived experience, Kimberly has developed a deep understanding of the non-linear nature of growth and healing. Her writing reflects a belief in self-compassion, honesty, and the quiet strength found in personal transformation.

At the heart of Kimberly's life are her children, who remain her greatest source of inspiration. They continually inform her sense of purpose and responsibility, reminding her that the most meaningful legacy is built through love, presence, and the lives we nurture. Through both education and writing, Kimberly seeks to encourage intentional living, resilience, and hope.

Made in the USA
Coppell, TX
20 June 2026

81301784R00121